Understanding Sade

"Understanding/graphic essay"
a collection directed by Luis de Miranda
© Max Milo éditions, Paris, 2023
www.maxmilo.com
ISBN 978-2-315-01266-4

Marie-Paule Farina
Yves Rouvière

Understanding Sade

Max Milo
COMPRENDRE/ESSAI GRAPHIQUE

"Ah, in Sade, at least, respect the scandal."
Maurice Blanchot,
La Raison de Sade, éditions de Minuit, 1963

Casanova had to respect this rule of good taste if he wanted to be invited to all the tables and tell his love stories.

Sade, let's say it right away, is in very bad taste: smells, flavors, "unpleasantly" mixed and "unpleasantly" repeated, too much philosophy for some, too much foutre for others, too much crap for most, too much length for all!

"Bad smell: a prejudice. All eliminations are disgusting - and why? Because they're foul? Why foul? They are not harmful... Disgust increases in proportion to refinement." Nietzsche has read Sade, and knows that "the mire of existence constitutes the best fertilizer", and that the **most refined of philosophies is nothing more than a transfiguration of a state of the body and a misunderstanding of the body.** What reader of *Justine* or *Juliette* could be unaware of this?

The widespread practice of extracts preserves us from excess and mixing... but what if what we are preserved from is precisely the greatest pleasure Sade offers us, what makes him forever different?

To exclude nothing and make everything more spiritual, more suave - perhaps this is the work of the Sadian still?

Vulgarity, stupidity and barbarity lie elsewhere, always on the side of the black, the dry, the serious, the sad, always in what excludes, separates and censors.

Who speaks an enigmatic, "wooden language"? The judge, inquisitor Dom Crispe Brutaldi Barbaribos de Torturentia. **Only one barbaric language, that in which one kills.** The other, the "vulgar", the language of insults, strikes only the air, and there was a time, a very long time ago, when EVERYTHING was recognized as a right, that of misfortune, that of the condemned to death.

Sade, the novelist, constructs an immense panoptikon in which he makes visible and dictable the repressed nature of all the philosophies of his time.

"The philosopher must say EVERYTHING, the philosopher must say what is *true*. Let's not forget Sade's injunction and the irony of the italics, which always underline the ridiculousness of his words.

Show a little modesty! Let's simply try to understand how Justine, Juliette, Léonore, Eugénie and so many others could have sprung from the imagination of a man who, between the ages of 27 and 74, spent just ten years in the open air and was twice sentenced to have his head cut off, even though there was no corpse in the closet, only an immense literary work and an immense mystification.

1. The Spoiled Child and the Trendy Young Man

WHAT IF IT ALL BEGAN AS A FAIRY TALE?

Donatien Alphonse François de Sade was born in Paris on June 2, 1740, Saint Blandine's Day, opposite the Luxembourg, in the capital's most beautiful palace. Fifty years later, as the character of his philosophical novel, Valcour, is ostensibly given his own biography, he takes an uncompromising look at the child he was and the "ineptitude" of his upbringing:

"Allied by my mother to all that was greatest in the Kingdom; held, by my father, to all that was most distinguished in the province of Languedoc; born in Paris in the bosom of luxury and abundance, I believed, as soon as I could reason, that nature and fortune were coming together to shower me with their gifts; I believed it because people were foolish enough to tell me so, and this ridicu-

"

lous prejudice made me haughty, despotic and angry; it seemed that everything had to yield to me, that the whole universe had to flatter my whims, and that it was up to me to form and satisfy them… [At the age of 4] I was sent to live with a grandmother in Languedoc, whose overly blind tenderness nurtured in me all the faults I have just confessed."

Sade's grandmother lived in a beautiful mansion in the center of Avignon, while his uncle, the abbé, lived in a mountain château in Saumane. The uncle, a friend of Voltaire, scholar and great lover of women, wrote a book on Petrarch and Laure de Sade, his ancestor, which had its moment of glory. In her company, the young Sade learned to dream of the love classes of those ancient times, of which Laure was the center. In his imagination, the link between the sweetness of a landscape, an era and a literature will live on forever. Clairwil's *Juliette* regardant la plaine lombarde expresses this nostalgia for a bygone past, and makes clear that she belongs to a time of volcanoes, calling for an explosive literature served up by mouths of fire. **The French Revolution, Etna and Vesuvius: these are the times and places of the Sadian novel.**

AT THE AGE OF 10, THE PARTY WAS OVER, and the Comte de Sade tore his son away from Provence and entrusted him to Abbé Amblet, a Genevoix tonsured cleric, and to the Collège Louis-le-Grand. There was still no trace of his mother. During the vacations, he went with Abbé Amblet to stay with his father's friend, the Duchesse de Longeville, who called him "my son" and developed with her other friend and "quasi-mother" (in Sade's own words), the Countess de Saint-Germain, his love of theater, poetry and, above all, his imaginary chivalry.

We can't understand Sade if we ignore the fact that he dreamed of love courts, troubadours, Petrarch, Laure and a society of gentleness and courtesy, where giving and feasting punctuated social relations.

At the age of 14, his father withdrew him from secondary school to enroll him in the chevau-légers school, a prestigious school if ever there was one, to which one was admitted only with an impressive number of quarters of nobility. The Seven Years' War began, and he took part in it, riding horses and taking on a redoubt with panache, but sleeping and playing instead of courting the officers on whom his career depended.

SOMETIMES HE FALLS IN LOVE TOO. His father followed him everywhere. In Paris, where he spent his winter quarters (in those days, when it was too cold, armies stopped fighting and everyone went home until spring), his father binged him on balls and female encounters, trying to deal with a homosexuality he suspected and worried about.

With Louis XV's Seven Years' War over and lost, Sade, like many other young officers, was idle.

A COMBUSTIBLE BODY RACING AHEAD, A LOVING HEART READY FOR ANY FOLLY, AND A REASON THAT ANALYZES AND REGRETS

AFTERWARDS, but only afterwards, all the foolish things that body and heart make people do: Sade is 20 years old and believes that one can only live in Paris, the most "civilized" city (that word has just been invented) in the world, among philosophers and enlightened people who have come back from all the bondieuseries and gothic beliefs.

Small parish schools did not do badly, and despite regional diversity, one in two French people could read before the Revolution.

Almanacs, the Blue Library and all the clandestine books, libels and other *philosophical books*, as the obscene and spicy books of the time were known, were a big hit.

Censorship exists, and so do bookshop inspectors, but never in any country, in any era - except perhaps our own, where the Internet has effectively replaced the always anonymous, always trashy libel - have rumors and fears been passed on at such speed.

In the Age of Enlightenment, people read the *Encyclopédie*, but they still believed in werewolves, poisoned waters and wells, and starved people blocking the grain trade. Those we had worshipped the day before were dragged through the mud.

Philosophy, libertinism and immorality are synonymous. To be in tune with the times, one must trample on childhood prejudices, weep in the theater by day, indulge in debauchery by night, and Sade wants, above all, to be in tune with the times!

THIS LITTLE WORLD OF ACTRESSES AND HANDSOME GENTLEMEN IS WATCHED OVER BY SARTINE, Louis XV's police lieutenant. Sade already had his "fly", the exempt de police Marais, who reported to Sartine, who in turn had to collect for the king, through the *"femmes du monde"* (as the madams were called), the juiciest details on the sexual behavior of private individuals. Young Sade's sexual behavior began to go off the rails, and so did his love life!

Doesn't this scatterbrain say he'll marry the person of his choice? His father, exasperated, drafts and distributes a small leaflet extolling the virtues of his son and his family, and manages to convince Monsieur le Président (of Parliament) and Madame Cordier de Montreuil that he is the ideal match for their daughter. After many comic adventures and a pox he cured with mercury at the home of his uncle the Abbé in Provence, Sade returned to Paris with a tuna pâté to make up for his late arrival (on the wedding day). He marries Marie-Pélagie, the Montreuil family's eldest daughter, whom he sees for the first time

Surveillé ?!
Mais constamment mon cher !
J'ai même ma propre mouche, ce
bon vieux Marais, certainement
planqué là-bas derrière à nous
épier !...
Rapport à Sartine dès ce
soir, sur la table du roi
demain à l'aube !
Et encore, vous
n'avez pas de paparazzi,
de vidéosurveillance, et
je ne parle même pas de
Facebook !
Tenez, nous allons être
" twittés" dans trente
secondes...

and realizes, but it's already too late, that the younger daughter would please him much more. The contract stipulated that his father would emancipate him (at 23, you're not yet an adult) and give up his position as colonel of the dragoons, and that the in-laws would pay a dowry, accommodation and all household expenses for five years.

In Paris, as in Échauffour in Normandy, **he plays comedy with his family, reads plays aloud, writes them, exercises his talent, which everyone recognizes, for "counterfeiting" and playing portraits, and imitates everyone "getting up, going to bed, having dinner"**. He knew how to make people laugh, was likeable and loved, but found his wife too cold and devout. Paris was here, he had more money than he'd ever had, and even though his father had moved in across the street, he was finally free of his guardianship.

He reads *Le Mercure* and the three almanacs: military, royal and entertainment, so he knows everything there is to know about the Court and the City, but he's hopelessly lacking in courtier spirit.

SIX MONTHS AFTER HIS MARRIAGE, HE WAS IMPRISONED FOR THE FIRST TIME AT VINCENNES BY ORDER OF THE KING, following the deposition of Jeanne Testard, a prostitute apprehended by Marais. His father ran to Fontainebleau, asked for the

King's pardon and obtained it. "Nothing has transpired," he wrote to his brother the Abbé, "and if it did, it would have to be denied. Sade was sent back to the country, and very quickly forgiven: "Since he was returned to us, we've been happy," assures the same Cordier mother-in-law, who, for the time being, is all sweetness and light.

The death of his father a few months later stunned him, and he decided to have children with his wife and play the role of model husband and father, but it didn't last long.

HE RESUMED HIS PARISIAN LIFE, SPENDING LAVISHLY, FREQUENTING THEATERS AND ACTRESSES, being in turn the lover of the Beaupré, the Colet and above all the beautiful Beauvoisin, for whom the richest and most titled men in Paris ruin themselves. He even brought the famous actress to Provence, to La Coste, and introduced her as his wife to all Provençal society invited to attend the shows and parties he gave at the château. His uncle the abbé, not the last to enjoy both the festivities and the company of Beauvoisin, informs his Parisian mother-in-law of all this, who suggests that he find some beautiful Provençal woman on the spot who would cost less and keep this son-in-law, who is squandering his inheritance and his wife's dowry, out of Paris.

1768: Arcueil affair. The Comte de Sade will no longer go to Fontainebleau to protect his son. Mrs de

Montreuil (the mother-in-law) intervenes for the first time. She requested and obtained from the king a lettre de cachet for the families. Letters de cachet were commonly used in all classes of society for offenses of "insurveillance": a husband could have his wife locked up, a wife her husband, and a parent his son or daughter. The aim was to bring about a change in behavior and escape the shame of a public trial. Sometimes there were a few abuses, but most of the time, within a few days or months, after asking for a confessor and taking communion, you'd be out, life would go back to normal, and nothing would filter through. This is what happened to Sade in 1763.

Times were changing, and despite the royal procedure and the lettre de cachet, which sent Sade, accompanied by Abbé Amblet, to Saumur prison, the matter was referred to Parliament, and newspapers and gazettes in France and abroad seized on the affair. The Comtesse de Saint-Germain wrote to Abbé de Sade: **"Public hatred for him is pushed beyond all expression... They want him to have done this crazy flogging as a mockery of passion...** The affair of M. de Fronsac and so many others adds to his own, and it is certain that for ten years it has been inconceivable what horrors have been committed by the people of the Court. For a fortnight now, there's been nothing but talk of this ridiculous affair."

2. A Man Lost in his Reputation

It was in Abbeville in 1766 that the Chevalier de la Barre was beheaded and burned with his copy of Voltaire's *Dictionnaire philosophique* nailed to his chest, after having undergone ordinary and extraordinary torture and having had his fist and tongue cut off. Paris was no Abbeville, and the mobilization of Voltaire and the philosophers' party was so strong at the time that there was never another conviction for blasphemy in France. Nonetheless, Sade was playing with fire, in 1763 as in 1768. Spanking a whore on Easter Sunday, the day of Christ's Passion, offering to confess and then sodomize her, and when she refuses, inflicting the martinet on her disguised as a pirate, is a very dangerous way of dressing up his sexuality. But it's not Sade who creates this cloak.

Pâques

"Those who believe in God, I send to the devil", says Durand in *Juliette*. This sentence, which could serve as an exergue to all of Sade's work, must, like so many others, be taken literally. Perhaps Sade can only cope with his homosexuality, the pleasure he takes in spanking and being spanked, and the pain he experiences with each ejaculation, by overplaying it all and integrating it into the script that, for centuries, the Church has provided for all Christians.

Sodomite, heretic, sorcerer not following "the right path" and doing everything backwards, it's all one for the Church and the very definition of the devil and his followers respecting nothing and laughing at everything.

In 1763, the deposition of Jeanne Testard describes even more blasphemous behavior: the young Sade, "trampling underfoot the prejudices of childhood", is said to have asked this young fanning worker engaged in prostitution to sodomize her and desecrate the host and crucifix, which she refused, but which nonetheless frightened her greatly! Let's not forget that a prostitute would be heavily punished if she confessed to having accepted, to use a Sadian metaphor, to be "seized" elsewhere than "in the vase of generation", perhaps this is what gives a slightly surreal aspect to the depositions of prostitutes "frightened" by the "diabolical" proposals of the young Sade.

Marais accompanied him and had to intervene in Saumur, Lyon, Moulins and Dijon, to protect him from the mob ready to "[gut] him to avenge the victims of [his] many crimes! In June, the whole of Paris flocked to the Tournelle criminal court to see M. de Sade, bareheaded and on his knees, being questioned by a magistrate. The doctor who examined Keller confirms Sade's version[1] who is sentenced to alms and returned to Pierre-Encize and the King's justice.

"I was too unhappy not to be guilty", Sade would later say, having returned to the hope he had at the time: that he would soon be forgotten in favor of another affair, another slander, another fashion. When Rousseau had just recounted in his *Confessions* that, as a child, he got his first erection from being spanked, how could we believe that Paris would condemn Sade for so long?

AFTER SEVEN MONTHS IN PRISON, Sade was released. His mother, the Dowager Countess, had intervened (he couldn't

---

1. The wounds were inflicted with a hammer and treated with an ointment. They were not "buttonholes" made with a knife and covered with wax, as the gazettes claimed.

believe it) and obtained exile on her lands from the King. But he was bored at La Coste, and his pregnant wife intervened to get her husband to come and support her.

Sade went up to Paris and stayed there for a while, wise and discreet. He read, wrote and still acted, even managing to get one of his plays placed and performed by the Bordeaux actors. In September 1769, he made a month-long trip to Holland, thanks to the sale to a publisher of a text (of which we know nothing) but which, he asserts in one of his letters, was an anonymous book in the tradition of Arétin's *Ragionamenti. Could* it be that Sade took notes on the sexual behavior of his contemporaries from the prostitutes he frequented? Or might he have completed the *Encyclopédie* project in a direction neglected by Diderot, but applying his method: describing the craftsman at work by making himself "an apprentice, as it were"? This is what the end of his letter from Vincennes to Sartine in 1763 might suggest:

"I also hope, Sir, that you will not inform my family of **the real reason for my detention**, as I would be lost without resources in their minds. I dare to make one more remark, Sir: the date of the **unfortunate book is** only June, I was married on the 17th of May and I can assure you that I only set foot in the said house in the month of June."

At Vincennes, struggling to write a verse tragedy and history books without much success, Sade confessed to Abbé Amblet that if he didn't succeed in writing "good" works to secure a new reputation, he would return to what his genius urged him towards, and which gave him a thousand times more pleasure than the noble genre : texts in the tradition of Arétin, the Venetian who advised a mother, worried about her daughter's future, to prefer the career of a whore to any other.

Let's not get ahead of ourselves: in 1770, Sade was still in the army and on his way to Fontenay-le-Comte in Poitou, where he had just been appointed captain of cavalry. As soon as he arrived, he was arrested by his commanding officer, who refused to receive an officer with his reputation. A duel and the end of his military life. In September 1771, he decided to return to his lands with his wife, children and sister-in-law.

3. La Coste. Marseille. Italy. Savoy: A Wicked Adventurer always Returning to the Fold

To understand Sade, you have to read his correspondence. Once we've read it, we know all about his little world and, apart from his in-laws, it includes only Provençals and a few Italian friends.

Present at this time, near him at La Coste, are :

Gaufridy, his childhood friend, the lawyer-notary who manages his estate and to whom he writes all his life, asking, in all tones, "Des sous! Des sous!", but also, in jest, to recount his hopes and fears, the main one being that he would betray him... which he does and has always done.

The abbé de Sade, the uncle, sees his nephew as a spirited horse who dabbles a little too much, and prefers to play both sides, serving the powerful mother-in-law, who is daily informed by both of them of her son-in-law's doings. Yet the abbé resembles his nephew, attending all his shows and parties and falling in love with Anne-Prospère, the young canoness sister-in-law!

Marie-Pélagie, the wife and friend, hates the bad spirit of the Provençals and calls her husband's friends "Monsieur", "Madame" and "Mademoiselle", even though she knows they hate it and find her "buttoned up like a parliament".

Gothon, the cook, "the most beautiful ass escaped from the mountains of Switzerland" to whom, according to her master, even his father-in-law, the president, would have paid homage. Gothon, so concerned about Sade's well-being that she sends him flowers and apricots from her garden as soon as she knows he's in prison in Aix, and has a hare shot to cook him a stew. Gothon wrote letters to Sade, who was imprisoned in Vincennes, in a style that varied according to the lovers who acted as her "dicteurs".

His valets: Latour, "le grand Latour", but above all Carteron dit la Jeunesse, a bad subject, lover of Gothon, copyist and favorite valet of Sade and his wife, who followed them to Paris to continue looking after his master's manuscripts in prison.

Paulet, the consul and later mayor of La Coste, Sade's friend, a Protestant like Gothon and his lover for a day, made him the butt of jokes by Sade and the curé de La Coste, amused to see these two Protestants sinning as happily as old Christians!

La Coste has a population of five hundred, half Catholic, half Protestant, meeting more at the cabaret than at the temple or church, and five hundred hectares, sixty of which belong to Sade. **Most of the peasants at La Coste, with whom Sade speaks Provençal (in this language, he says, I only know "the low comic"),** own their own land and raise silkworms. They all agree to let everyone have their own bodies (as long as they don't knock up their daughters) and to hate the people of Aix and their parliamentarians even more, if that's possible, than the uptight Parisians. In 1545, the king's troops had stormed the Vaudois at La Coste, and the lord of Oppède, president of the Aix parliament, had finished the job.

The memory of Mérindol, of Cabrières (the Provençal Saint-Barthélémy) is still alive in the village and in the work of a Sade who always vomited "religious wars that killed millions when they weren't worth the blood of a bird".

Sade was also a friend of Vidal (the canon of Oppède), who later hid him in his home and with whom he was to leave for Spain to exploit a gold mine.

To complete the circle of Sade's friends, all that was missing was one figure, and not the least, Marie-Dorothée

Rousset, whom he would call "ma petite sainte", "ma petite bête", "ma petite compote", because her letters made him laugh so much at Vincennes that he kept them as a sweet for his dessert. "Monsieur le fagot d'épines" is what she called him, and it's true that in those days, Sade quickly caught fire: it was "the energy of the Sades", he said, so much preferable to "the morgue of the Montreuil" that his sons, to his great despair, seemed to have inherited.

No sooner had he arrived at La Coste than he embarked on a major project, planting cherry trees in his park, organizing a theater festival to which he invited the whole neighborhood, and finally, in the middle of it all, on the pretext of collecting leases, he and Latour went off to Marseilles to have "a party" with four prostitutes. We eat aniseed candies, spiced with cantharides, to get in shape. One of the prostitutes, who had eaten more than the others, became ill, her landlady alerted the police and, before Sade and Latour had even returned to La Coste, the maréchaussée were hot on their heels, warning Sade that he was about to be arrested because a prostitute had died. Terrified, he fled with Latour to Italy. Less than two months later, they were condemned to death by the Aix parliament for sodomy and poisoning (the prostitutes, who were still alive, had lodged a complaint only for poisoning!)

In the heart of the Age of Enlightenment, on the Place Saint-Louis in Aix, Sade's effigy had its head cut off, Latour's was hanged (the egalitarian guillotine had not yet arrived) and both were burned, their ashes scattered to the wind.

Sade was contumacious, lived in Italy for a while, then came back, left with his sister-in-law, who left him, and returned to La Coste without him after his first infidelity. He finally fled to Savoy, where his mother-in-law had him arrested and imprisoned. He escaped from the "Savoyard Bastille", returned to La Coste and lived with his wife for a while.

THE "PETITES FILLES" SCANDAL ERUPTS: the father of Justine, one of the "servants" he has recruited in Lyon with their titular madam Nanon (quite legally, according to Sade), comes to make a scene at the château and shoots Sade at point-blank range. The shot doesn't go off, but it scares everyone. Paulet finally manages to lecture a man who, writes Sade to Gaufridy, couldn't believe his daughter was alive and kept telling anyone who would listen that if he killed the Marquis, he'd been assured he'd be safe!

Goupil, the bookshop's inspector, whose trip from Paris has been paid for by Madame President, has already, in Sade's absence, terrorized Gothon and his wife and taken all the papers from his study in the hope of recovering not only letters that might compromise the youngest daughter, but also, as in Savoie and Fort de Miolans, libels against the family and "manuscripts against morals".

It's not just Sade's body that's combustible: "**Your style burns paper,**" says his wife, who calls Sade "vouvoie" when she's angry with him. Why doesn't he listen to her? I'm **told you'd be out long ago if you'd change your style**", she repeated to him, in vain, in Vincennes and the Bastille!

Informed by his mother-in-law of his mother's state of health, Sade went up to Paris with his wife, Jeunesse and Justine (who wouldn't leave them), and, as soon as he arrived, was arrested in his room, in his wife's presence, by Marais. His mother had been dead for a fortnight, and his mother-in-law had persuaded Louis XVI to reconduct her son-in-law's lettre de cachet.

4. "A Rage from Vincennes," "Why make Unhappy Those you Cannot make Good?"

Is he locked up for a week? A month? A year? That's the only question he asks his wife to answer as soon as she's allowed to write to him. "I assure you that you will not stay a day longer than necessary." This kind of answer drives Sade mad, but he absolutely refuses to believe her when she tells him she knows nothing about it. He begs her to tell him the truth, but can't bear the thought that his lettre de cachet bears no date. If it did, he'd just have to smash his head against the wall.

After sixteen months in Vincennes, he made the "voyage to Aix", still in the company of Marais. Parliament overturns his judgment in absentia, the prostitutes testify, and **he is sentenced not for sodomy and poisoning, but for "outrageous libertinism", to alms and a three-year ban from Marseille.** He was happy... for a short time. Marais picks him up in the middle of the night to take him back to Vincennes, as his mother-in-law has not had the lettre de cachet annulled. On the way, he escapes Marais and his brother, and returns to La Coste, where he is feted by his friends. A month later, he was kidnapped again, at night, at La Coste, by four Parisian exempts (including Marais, of course) and six men from the Salon maréchaussée, all paid by his mother-in-law.

THE VINCENNES DUNGEON IS NOT A THREE-STAR PRISON, WHATEVER PEOPLE MAY SAY. Cell n° 6, where Sade is locked up, is tiny with a dirt floor, and you have to cohabit in the dust with rats and mice.

What Sade suffered most from was loneliness and the lack of air and walks, but at least now he knew to whom he owed all his misfortunes.

"My life is sold. I'm being served through a trap door like the lunatics."

"My mother-in-law is afraid I'll stage it. You have to leave the Calibans to Shakespeare, they don't do well in our theater."

"She treats my possessions like cabbages from her garden."

What is this "Vincennes rage" that makes him "a wretch who sees nothing, hears nothing and for

whom letters are the only horoscopes where he believes he will find his fate?"

We'd have to quote all his letters to understand the transformation of the dashing young marquis into "Monsieur le 6". **Monsieur le 6** sees strange growths appearing in his body and mind, for which he would need to consult "some doctor of the soul", but he has none at his disposal, and when he consults them because he is beginning to go blind, he is advised against reading and writing: shouldn't he rather be doing network or knitting, like at Bicêtre?

So it's up to him to find the means - his means - not only to survive, but to live as well as possible, without worrying about a thing: "That's all there is to it. Everything is blasé! Everything is blunt. Your shortest course is to let me rest.

Happy stoicism" is the philosophy of this new Sade, who enters the resistance.

First, despite criticism and "teasing", he read and wrote non-stop ("I want to do it day and night, and I don't want to do anything else"), enjoying all the little pleasures that remained.

He loves sweets and will send his wife shopping lists. Why should he deprive himself of cologne and pretty notebooks? Chocolate, figs, strawberries, butter from

Brittany or cupcakes? What connection is there between the fibers in his stomach and the Salic law? None, so let him enjoy such an innocent pleasure in peace.

Next, he will claim "rights", not those of man, but those of "a menagerie animal": to be clean, to eat proper food, to have his cage swept, to be able to sleep without being disturbed by mice or untimely night-time entrances from anyone.

He'll also try to poke fun at the stupidity of the "text scribblers" who read and censor all his letters. He'll even make "Jacques le scribouilleur" a great man for his constancy in vice. When reading Sade's letters, always bear in mind the third party who stands between him and his wife, punishing him for all his deviations from "style" by depriving him of visits, walks and paper. Milli Rousset is the only one who dares to address both Sade and those who get hot under the collar by reading his letters. When she writes him "foutaises" (nonsense) in Provençal, she translates it for them, which makes Sade die laughing, as he only asks for one thing: to be distracted from Vincennes.

"The first time I entered Vincennes, I thought I was in Liliput because all the rules were so tiny, and I preferred to think I was 12 years old rather than that the people who ran it all had them.

"My pranks are good for entertaining children, but what am I here for, if not a child?"

As a child, an animal, a Jew condemned to pluck out his eyes to read the Scriptures and find in his wife's letters the number of his destiny and the date of his release, Sade discovered that "nature gives very singular inspirations to a being abandoned to himself and deprived of society". Would he begin to believe in dreams and miracles? "This miracle (if it exists) is no more singular, and even much less so than the inspiration it gives animals about the plants that are beneficial to them.

Diderot at Vincennes, Casanova at Les Plombs (they too) cast spells to find the date of their release. If there's one path you should never take to understand Sade, it's the one that separates him from other men. *Sade, mon prochain"*, said Klossowski, "Sade, mon semblable" (*Sade, my* fellow man), I'm content to say of a man of unfailing mental health, whose courage of spirit is the first of his qualities.

Sade, long before Michel Tournier, long before Gilles Deleuze, had discovered that his solitude

condemned Robinson to become a pervert, but Robinson's solitude was in the wilderness, Sade in an enclosed space, and all his work explored the monstrosities that enclosed spaces give birth to.

"Sade is the horror of nature… There isn't a tree in his work," remarks Flaubert. Flaubert gets to the heart of the matter, but Sade, the Sade man, can only live in open spaces; he weeps when he learns that one night the thirty cherry trees he had planted at La Coste have been cut down; in spring, he needs flowers more than books, and his wife brings him flowers when she visits him, But his libertines only operate in enclosed spaces, sheltered by the high walls of castles and convents, or on the "lips" of still-active volcanoes that sterilize all the land around them.

"I have been guided by this axiom of natural law: to do myself justice whenever it is denied me."

Cross-outs and erasures have replaced wheels; it's at the corners of his wife's letters that he hurts himself, it's his mind that is attacked by encrypting everything that reaches him and letting him imagine the worst if he doesn't get wise and modify his style and philosophy. "I'm locked up for my shortcomings; it's the best way to make me cherish them for the rest of my life." Perhaps, but from the outset the Sadian enterprise goes further, and not to forget the goal he pursues and will pursue against all odds, or rather, on the contrary, against walls and chains, he writes on the bookmark he sees every day since it serves as his bookmark:

"If only some animals from the other world, who will no doubt soon return to it, hadn't figured out that nothing destroys vices like not seeing the sun. An opinion too barbarically Gothic for M. de Sade not to do his homeland the service of proving its absurdity."

The most immoral and scandalous work ever written was written by someone who was locked up to make him "think"!

Vous avez imaginé
Faire merveille, je le parierais,
en me réduisant à une abstinence
atroce sur le péché de la chair.
Eh bien, vous vous êtes trompés : vous avez
échauffé ma tête, vous m'avez fait
former des fantômes qu'il faudra
que je réalise.

5. Jonah, or the Prophet, in Spite of Himself

SADE WAS A PROPHET, A ROLE IN WHICH HE WAS NOT OFTEN IMAGINED, and yet, ten years before the Revolution, he saw the absence of fairness as a source of further misfortune which, added to poverty, could only lead to upheaval.

The tranquil philosopher," he writes, "removed from this stormy sea and calculating from such misguidance the infallible and imminent consequences for the state that suffers them, will he not be able to become as good a prophet as Jonah?

VINCENNES AND THE BASTILLE BECOME THE WHALE OF THIS SADE-JONAS, A PROPHET IN SPITE OF HIMSELF, like Jonah who refused to go to Nineveh to announce their impending doom to men who no longer recognized their left from their right. Nineveh will be saved, not Sodom, where there were too few righteous, but the prophet Sade is a pessimist, and at the end of the *120 Days of Sodom,* he holds out the green thread of the Apocalypse's surviving elect to the executioners and those who serve them:

"On March 1, everything that's left is shipped out in detail. The friends decide to give a green ribbon to everything that is to be brought back to France on condition that they lend a hand in the torture of the rest."

Diderot looks for the date of his release on the pages of his Platon, and Sade on a *Fleur des Saints* where, for each saint, he gives a number.

His wife sometimes writes to him in "milk" or "lemon", a kind of friendly ink, what he considers trifles and never what matters to him: the date of his release. He's sure it's written down somewhere, and don't let her tell him otherwise - this illusion is necessary for his survival, and "you can't take a rattle away from a child" - but let her stop being the instrument of his torment, and stop speaking in riddles and word games to be deciphered.

He reads Father Massillon's sermons, "he's not a bigot who talks", and yet Louis XIV didn't listen to him and killed millions while he preached gentleness, so what's the point of sermons?

He also read or leafed through the many volumes of *Cérémonies religieuses* which, as "curiosities", described the most exotic religious practices. He would leaf through these books at La Coste, with his wife, to distract themselves during their long winter evenings.

Need we remind you of the most common use of the *Lives of the Saints* in Jesuit schools? Historians, who are often witty, point out that surviving copies open on the same page, on June 2, the day of the martyrdom of Saint Blandine, depicted as always naked, pierced by arrows, with her breasts cut off, delivered to a bull, and so on. It was **in religious martyrologies, Christian or otherwise, that Sade sought the "inspiration" for The *120 Days of Sodom*, and it wasn't he who discovered that one could warm one's head by recounting horrors!**

Like Hitchcock, Sade likes to make one or more more or less discreet and unexpected appearances in what he calls (wherever he wrote them): *my Bastille books.* **In *Sodome*, he chooses his patron saint, and his choice is final.**

"Everyone preaches to his own saint," says Dolmancé in *Philosophy in the Boudoir*, but which saint is Sade preaching to?

President Curval (the judge) spoke of him, Sade, **on** November 23, to his friend the Duc de Blangis:

"Everyone knows the story of the Marquis de... who, as soon as he was told of the sentence that would burn him in effigy, pulled his vit out of his breeches and cried out: "Foutredieu! Here I am at the point where I wanted to be, here I am covered in opprobrium and infamy, let me go, let me go, I've got to get it off my chest!" And he did so at once."

Need it be said that ***The 120 Days of Sodom*, this heretical martyrology, describes an upside-down world whose sole purpose is to "demoralize[2] the torment"?**

What "moral" do the two friends draw from this story?

Oh, what an enigma that man is!" said the duke.

- Yes, my friend," says Curval. And this is what makes a man of great spirit say that it was better to fuck him than to understand him."

We who seek to understand Sade should not be demoralized[3] right from the start of our undertaking. Sade thinks exactly the opposite, and **if he sets this whole scene on November 23, St. Clement's Day, it's because this**

---

2.   First meaning: to make immoral (*Littré*)

3.   Second meaning: to take away morale, courage (*Littré*)

saint is the only one to whose imitation he calls all those who think "we must lock up to soften" and "fuck rather than understand".

A lesson in clemency is better than a lesson in despotism, but then again, isn't Sade just another lesson-giver, describing the criminal practices of decrepit, imbecilic "ciphers", "maltôtiers", "financiers", "robins" and "magistrates", just so they can stop deluding themselves?

"And the idol, entirely stripped by his care, would offer to the enlightened multitude only the crude and disgusting matter of which it is composed"?

6. A World Turned Upside Down: From Hell to Carnival

Only the fabulous warms the head, only the fabulous allows us to escape the fears of the night, for the devils and ogres it gives birth to terrify, but… from a distance. **Sade, in the night of his prison, invents the black novel, the blackest ever written, and recounts without "gassing" the way in which anthropophagous and scatophagous "great men" recharge their batteries in the seraglio offered to their lust.** Fear not, these men are cowards, recoiling from a fight on equal terms, and even the weakest but most resolute child, with his laughter, would send them fleeing to the other end of the earth. Sade makes this clear from the outset in his portrayal of the Duc de Blangis, the "colossus" who leads the whole gang to the Château de Silling.

Already, he was following the advice he would later give to the young novelist: "No one is forcing you into the trade you're doing; but if you undertake it, do it well. Don't adopt it as an aid to your existence, it would have the pallor of hunger."

In 1783, Sade began to regain the strength to laugh and the taste for jokes, and the work he wrote would never be a work of resentment born of sad passions. A note from him, written at midnight, simply says to his wife:

"I'm writing to you out of the gaiety of my imagination and give you a big hug."

The day before, he'd told her that if he didn't receive the books he'd been waiting for to continue writing theater and history, he'd take the opportunity to embark on a great novelistic suite that would give him much more pleasure.

In 1784, at night and "naked" (as usual), he was transferred to the Bastille. There, between two stones in the wall of his cell, he wrote and hid the twelve-meter-long scroll of The *120 Days of Sodom*. Or rather, it was there that he wrote the first part, covering the month of November, the rest being a catalog of abuse, certainly unreadable, in which Sade seems to pursue only two objectives: not to repeat himself and to go ever further in horror.

Sade lost this manuscript, which was sold with the Bastille stones, preserved, it seems, in Germany and first published in 1931. Sade could have rewritten it and published it, but he didn't, and not without good reason.

BEWARE, THEN, OF THE VERY SPECIAL STATUS OF THIS TEXT, which, when first published, was presented and read as a catalog of all perversions. Already, Gilbert Lely (it's thanks to him and Jean-Jacques Pauvert that we can read Sade today) noticed an "error": the omnipresence of "coprolagnic aberration carried to its last excess", which we'll call, preferring Rabelaisian vocabulary: **scatophagy, which Rabelais, like Sade, makes the characteristic of all powers.** Is it so incomprehensible today that Aristophanes inaugurates by mocking the disciples of Aesculapius, that Rabelais goes on to present a monk as a "chewing-shit" who feeds on everyone's sins, and Sade a judge as a "fouille merde" and an "mange merde"? No, but it is "vulgar", and as Kundera rightly says: **"In France, to say of someone that he is 'vulgar', especially if he is a novelist, is really the supreme insult."** Voltaire, for the same reason, wanted to keep only a few pages of Rabelais and discard the rest, much to the dismay of Diderot, who compared Rabelais to the immense statue of Saint-Christophe, between whose legs all Parisians passed to enter the cathedral. To put it plainly, and Diderot's language was already very clear: my old man, neither you nor I have "got to his balls".

The statue of Saint-Christophe has long since disappeared, and generations of twentieth-century high-school students have learned from the textbooks of Messieurs Lagarde et Michard that Diderot was a vulgar writer who lacked the (French, of course) "spirit" of Voltaire. "Plebeian, sensual, talkative and demonstrative, Diderot lacks tact and delicacy."

And that's how literary history is written, just like any other, and that's what Sade will mock too, taking care not to challenge the illegitimate "false" with a legitimate but equally peremptory and indisputable "true".

In one of his *Seminars*, Lacan writes, not without humor: "It's not me, it's Saint John." All discourses of power are discourses written from the point of view of God or his saints. **What Sade shows is that there is no narrative without a subject, without desire, without a body.** Long before Nietzsche, long before Freud, Sade was the bearer of this "great suspicion". The origin of **gai savoir** is the same from Rabelais to Nietzsche via Sade: **"We are not thinking frogs, gutless objectifying devices." Let's beware of the "objective mind", "half-philosophers who analyze everything without ever understanding anything".**

There are sick philosophers just as there are sick critics, and they can be recognized by the fact that they hide behind objectivity and anonymity.

By turning Sade into a novelist who, in the middle of the 18th century, reintroduced "low comedy" into literature, a genre that is still present in popular language today, aren't I doing him and myself a disservice? It would be easier to understand why I belong to the fan club of a *serial killer* and "confess", like so many others, that Sade's sadism as developed in *The 120 Days of Sodom* fascinated me and brought me to the brink of the abyss and suicide, rather than simply hearing myself say that I laughed when I read, for example, the account of the perversion of a parliamentarian (surely from Aix-en-Provence, these garlic-scented hiccups give him away), given aloud and "in the tone of good company" by La Duclos, the madam on duty, in that November[4].

LET'S SKIP THE PRELIMINARIES AND GET TO THE HEART OF "PERVERSION":

"He stretched out his legs, I placed myself on a lower seat next to him, and having drawn from his fly a hint

---

4.   The month in which the story of the *120 Days of Sodom* begins.

of very flabby vit instead of a real member, I set about, despite my repugnance, sucking this beautiful relic, hoping it would take on a little consistency in my mouth: I was wrong. As soon as I had collected it, the libertine began his operation; he devoured rather than ate the pretty little fresh egg I had just made for him: it was a matter of three minutes, during which his extensions, his movements, his contortions, announced to me a most ardent and expressive voluptuousness. But no matter how hard he tried, nothing came of it, and the naughty little tool, after crying out of spite in my mouth, withdrew more ashamed than ever, leaving his master in the despondency, abandonment and exhaustion that are the fatal consequence of great voluptuousness".

Convinced by this tale, Durcet, renouncing not the trappings but "the turds of youth", realizes that he will be best served by his old friend Curval, the president of the court, etc.

Even in February, the month of murderous passions, the last circle of hell can turn out to be the month of the most classic carnivalesque practices. Women who become servants or beasts for food, valets who take the place of masters, incongruous marriages and couplings.

"Part Four: Establish [Sade the writer always uses the formal form of address when speaking to himself] that everything changes that month; that the four wives are repudiated; that Julie, however, has found favor with the bishop, who has taken her into his home as a servant, but that Aline, Adélaïde and Constance are without fire or place. In the case of Adélaïde and Aline, they are sleeping in the stables of the animals intended for food." On February 12, Augustine, daughter of a Languedoc baron kidnapped by madams and cutthroats to enter the seraglio of the four libertines, forgetting the nobility of her birth, allies herself with a "subaltern whippersnapper" who offered her an escape. "We realize that there was a small beginning of a general riot among the fouteurs subalternes."

JULY 2, 1789: FROM INSIDE THE BASTILLE, SADE HEARS THE REVOLT OF THE FAUBOURG SAINT-ANTOINE, **takes a long tin pipe with a funnel at one end to empty out, shall we say, his sewage, and using it as a megaphone, shouts that the throat is being slit in the Bastille.** Like Sodom's Augustine, to save his life, Sade, despite his real fear of popular ferocity, attempts his first alliance with the faubourg and "les fouteurs subalternes"… and it works!

How could he not be confirmed in the idea that everything that happened to him was just a farce, when this act of anger (perhaps simply due to the fact that his walk had been suppressed), after having sent him, the very next day and for nine months, to Charenton with "fols et épileptiques" (fools and epileptics), assured him consideration and a reputation as a prophet in the Paris of 1790, where the suppression of the lettres de cachet finally gave him back his freedom? Restif de la Bretonne, who fifteen years earlier had made him a "vivisector", describes him, with just as much concern for the truth, carried by the crowd, white beard in battle, emerging on July 14 from the Bastille - where he had unfortunately not been for ten days - surrounded by the heads of his jailers planted on pikes.

7. Free at Last!

"You have to have known the situation of someone who breaks his fetters to be in a position to return it; it's a new air you breathe, it's new sensations you experience; it's an enormous weight you get rid of." When Sade says this in *Aline et Valcour*, we take him at his word!

Having been imprisoned in the Bastille no longer disgraces, quite the contrary, Sade tells Gaufridy and asks him to let the whole province know, but above all he asks him for money, and right away, because he's naked, and all the more so because his wife no longer wants to receive him, she who a few years earlier wrote to him: **"If your poor head didn't sometimes wander off to write unseemly things, you'd be the perfect being, but you'll always be perfect for me."** Never say "always" when you're a weathervane who falls for the first confessor who comes along and hands over all her husband's manuscripts for him to burn. Later, the virtuous younger son would also burn all his father's posthumous manuscripts.

At the age of 50, an obese Sade appeared on the Paris pavement, a Paris he found hard to recognize after thirteen years of imprisonment, and which immediately offered him the abolition of censorship, which had just been voted in, as well as a brand new status, that of "author of invention".

But first, Sade felt the need to talk, to see people. He was one of the Parisians who flocked to theaters, both old and new, to see the "English dramas" that were all the rage: black, black, corpses, monks. He recycles his plays, tries to give them the tone of the day, manages to get the actors to read them, obtains a year's subscription in one theater, and has one of his plays performed in another, but unluckily, for the first time, some of the audience are wearing red bonnets and making such a racket that the play is interrupted.

He is received by Mr. and Mrs. de Clermont-Tonnerre. M. de Clermont Tonnerre, his cousin's husband, was an elected member of the Assemblée Nationale, over which he presided twice. He led the "monarchien" party, and at the time, Sade too seemed to favor an English-style system, a constitutional monarchy with two chambers. He wrote

this to Gaufridy, who asked for his opinion on all these innovations, pointing out that **he was now a "man of letters" and, as such, wrote so many speeches for one party or another that he no longer knew what he thought himself!**

He met Madame Quesnet, an actress twenty years his junior, who remained with him until her death in 1814. He moved in with her on rue Neuve-des-Mathurins, and led, he says, the quiet life of a priest in his presbytery! He was an active member of the Place Vendôme section, paid his taxes, attended his section meetings and, above all, continued to write, having the immense pleasure of being able to "hot-read" his manuscripts in Constance.

First of all, he doesn't write his memoirs, which would have been a bestseller at a time when the stones of the Bastille are being snatched up and the smallest fragments made into earrings and medallions. Why doesn't he? *Aline et Valcour*, his philosophical novel, boasts, in its signature ("Written in the Bastille one year before the French Revolution by M. le marquis de Sade"), in its preface, its editor's notice and notes, this brand-new reputation as a victim of despotism with gifts of clairvoyance "worthy of arousing public curiosity", but, very strangely, Sade published it not in 1790 but in 1795, and right from his preface, insists on its gap with the present:

"How could the work written seven years ago be on the agenda?"

Whatever Sade may say, not all his books were written at the Bastille, or if they were, it was in a very different form to the one we have before us today. **The Bastille was the kitchen where Sade did his apprenticeship, from which he drew his spices, his ideas and, in a way, his inaugural speech as chef and "amphitryon offering six hundred dishes to our appetite", but all his novels were published under the Revolution,** with the exception of one very special one, *La Marquise de Gange*, for which he made it clear in 1813: "This is not a novel."

8. The Ledger of Reputations

LET'S NOT CONFUSE SADE AND CHODERLOS DE LACLOS: their paths were exactly the opposite. *Les Liaisons dangereuses* was published in 1782. During the French Revolution, Choderlos de Laclos worked for Philippe Égalité, fought in the war and held important positions in the bloodthirsty Commune, at the bishop's palace, before being imprisoned like Sade at Picpus in 1794 and, like him, escaping the scaffold. They rubbed shoulders in difficult times, but never spoke of each other. **Sade is the novelist, the only novelist of the Revolution**, and this, of course, displeases all those who, today as yesterday, are bent on grooming the Revolution to make it presentable from start to finish, and speak of Sade, when they do, as if he were an aristocrat lost in a period that was not his own.

"Infamous or divine, our marquis cannot be a citizen.

MARAT
LEPELETIER

**And yet, he was, and "wet from the neck up":
public writer at the service of the public, editor of
all the projects and motions of his section in Place
Vendôme, which became the very "popular" Piques
section. It was even he who wrote and delivered,
on a crowded square, the "Discours aux mânes"
(speech to the spirits) of Marat, who had just been
assassinated!** Marat, l'Ami du peuple, "irritated that
the title of philanthropist should be contested, when he
claimed only a small number of heads (273,000) to save
all the others". (I'm quoting Marat, and the figure is his.)
Apologizing for this kind of great man was Sade's specialty,
so how could he lend his pen and his voice to his section
without adding his little bell?

"Frenchmen, always honor and admire your great men,
and if posterity ever accused you of some error, wouldn't
your sensitivity be your excuse? The Romans, by a severe
law, required a long interval between the death of a famous
man and his eulogy, let us not imitate this rigor, it would
cool our virtues.

A kitchen boy in the revolutionary kitchen, Sade, like
so many kitchen boys before him, took a dip in the soup
before serving it at the master's table.

THE ANCIEN RÉGIME? SADE, IN HIS OWN WAY, DENOUNCED
ITS DESPOTISM AND ABUSES IN *Sodome*, where he had the Duc

de Blangis say: "But the Ancien Régime is dead, and **Sade never denounces the evils of yesterday, but always those of today, if we are willing to admit that his apologies do more harm than good. In any case, he only laughs at those who are on stage at the moment they are, or, as we must do, right at the end of their performance.**

FOR THE TIME BEING, SADE ENJOYED HIS NEWFOUND FREEDOM, but despite the abolition of censorship, his first publication *Justine et les malheurs de la vertu* was anonymous. Maurice Heine had fun re-establishing, from Sade's drafts, the first version of the little tale of Justine and Juliette her sister, written in the Bastille in just a few dozen pages, which served as the matrix for the hundreds of pages of *Justine* of 1791 and the thousands of pages of *La Nouvelle Justine ou les malheurs de la vertu followed by L'Histoire de Juliette, sa sœur et les prospérités du vice*, which appeared from 1797 to 1800. What's certain, from the outset, is that the little passage I'm about to quote from the 1791 *Justine is not to be* found there. Let's not forget that, in 1791, it was the virtuous Justine, "an entirely sentimental individual", who recounted her adventures, and the whole flavor of this text lies in the abundance of metaphors she invented to keep her tale in good taste.

"But what new weapons would, alas, present themselves to me! Julien and La Rose, who were undoubtedly heated by all this, also stripped of their breeches, stepped forward with pike in hand... Oh, Madame, nothing like this has ever stained my eyes before."

These sans-culottes, pike in hand, corresponded perfectly to the spirit of the times, which made them the very embodiment of virility in the face of the aristocratic "bande à l'aise", but it was the bande à l'aise who were writing in 1790, and the titles of the two-cent books to be found in the galleries of what was still the Palais-Royal, but was soon to become the Palais-Égalité, are unambiguous in this respect: *Les Fouteurs de bon goût à l'Assemblée nationale, Recueil de chansons foutro-critico-energico-lubriques, dédiées à tous les crasseux disciples de saint François, par un bande à l'aise,* and it was against this backdrop that Sade brought out the peppery, spicy novel his publisher had asked for, but which he would classify as "wordless erotica".

IN 1793, CENSORSHIP WAS RE-ESTABLISHED, ROBESPIERRE AND SAINT-JUST BROUGHT THE SANS-CULOTTES BACK INTO LINE, AND OPEN-AIR BANQUETS, BINGE DRINKING AND REFERENCES TO RABELAIS ALL CAME TO THE FORE. The aim was to "give a just idea of happiness", and strangely enough, it was the *Nouvelle Justine* of 1797, using all the "words of art", that was to put the "foutre" in all the right places, and the sans-culottes back where they belonged. No more pikes, no more breeches pulled down to frighten Justine without doing her much harm, Julien and the Rose are content to take our inusable Justine, to the Bishop's Palace, to their master of torture, who, incidentally, reads *La Philosophie dans le boudoir* before officiating as a judge. It's another of Sade's thumbs down, another way of pulling the wool over our eyes and playing with our image of him!

At the end of *Sodom*, Sade writes to himself: "Never make the four friends do anything that hasn't been told to them" by one of the four historians. These men of a fading power listen and reproduce, but are no longer capable of inventing new practices or justifying their own. Philosophy is so foreign to them that, on the contrary, they foresee a fine for anyone who doesn't go to bed drunk and "manages to have even a glimmer of reason".

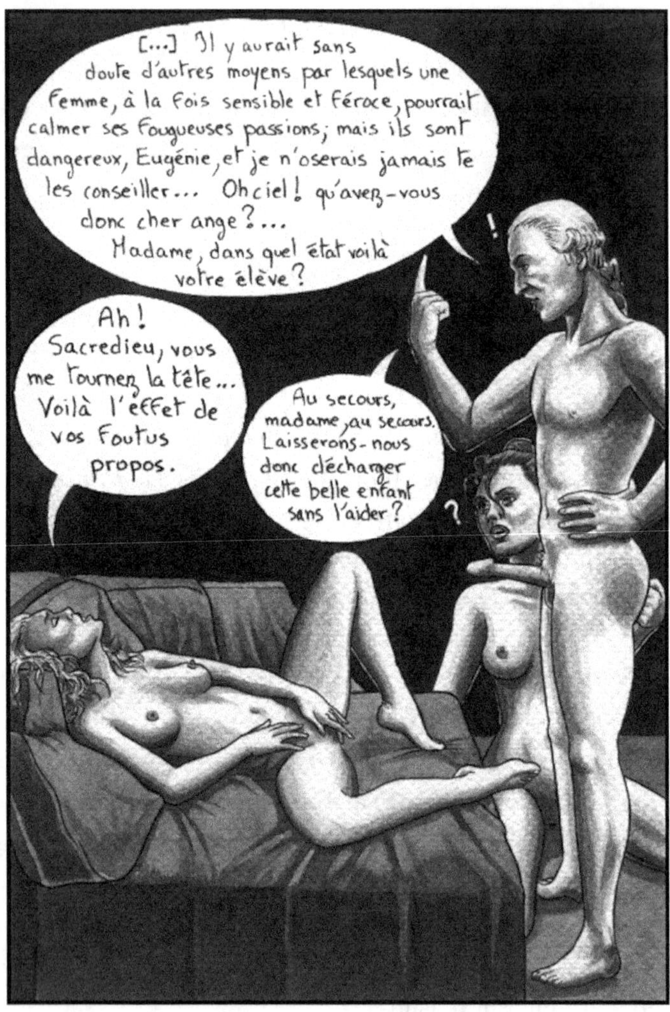

[...] Il y aurait sans doute d'autres moyens par lesquels une femme, à la fois sensible et féroce, pourrait calmer ses fougueuses passions; mais ils sont dangereux, Eugénie, et je n'oserais jamais te les conseiller... Oh ciel! qu'avez-vous donc cher ange?... Madame, dans quel état voilà votre élève?
Ah! Sacredieu, vous me tournez la tête... Voilà l'effet de vos foutus propos.
Au secours, madame, au secours. Laisserons-nous donc décharger cette belle enfant sans l'aider?

The men and women Sade now presents speak, discuss, justify themselves, try to convince, and we don't find this in the little tale written at the Bastille, or in *Sodom*. In a way, the situation has been reversed: Juliette's biographer is now the narrator. At Château de Silling, the duke, the financier, the bishop and the president of the court, "those leeches always on the lookout for public calamities", fed on the private lives of ordinary people. In the great series of novels that Sade set out to construct from 1791 onwards, it is he, Sade, who will feed his readers with accounts of the private lives of public men and women (the pun is not out of place!), but these men and women of power are all great reasoners, are all philosophers! **This is the hallmark of Sadie's work, the irresistible transition from the most serious philosophical discourse to the immediate realization of its effect not on minds, but on bodies.**

Bandole, to whom Justine asks what "titles of authority" he has over her, simply replies, showing the state of his vit: "Je bande et je veux foutre" ("I'm hard and I want to fuck"), and unfortunately it would seem that, for Sade, everyone holds the speech that allows them to justify their dominant passion and ultimately resembles Bandole, minus the frankness.

9. Is There such a Thing as Sadist "Thought"?

"Machiavellian", "sadistic", the French language has united Machiavelli and Sade in the hit parade of evil. Althusser, in revealing the "rule of method" followed by Machiavelli, provides an equally pertinent key to understanding Sade: **"Thinking in extremes… in a position, where to make thought possible, one occupies the place of the impossible."**

No one can subscribe to the theses, to all the theses defended by the Sadian libertines, and yet they seem to be unfailingly rational.

"In this case, it's another philosopher, Clément Rosset, who reminds us that Sade is, above all, a novelist and that "Sadian 'thought' is purely a literary effect". Certainly, but if Sade's work offers "all genders, all ages, all passions, all debaucheries, all crimes", it also offers a walk through all the sophisms that the mind produces under the dictation of the body's impulses.

"The food we propose here to our reader is none other than human nature", asserts novelist Fielding in *Tom Jones*, and to endure such food, one must, according to Sade, have "stomach" and vomit nothing as unassimilable or disgusting, for the police are always and above all a police of taste.

To REDISCOVER THE INVENTIVENESS OF AN ARISTOPHANES OR A SOCRATES, AFTER CENTURIES OF APOLOGIES FOR LOVE, PERHAPS WE NEED TO GORGE OURSELVES TO OUR HEART'S CONTENT ON APOLOGIES FOR VICE AND CRIME? Juliette, having gone through all the branches of the tree of crime, is visited one night, in a dream, by an angel who has come to announce incomprehensible virtues that, when she wakes up, she feels a kind of nostalgia for. Perhaps this is what makes her dare to trust and love Durand?

Let's not fear this return of the virtuous repressed, for contrary to what the great Lacan said in his *Kant and Sade*, this is not a return to the Law in its most castrating form.

"You're the best thing for my happiness, you're the woman I've been looking for, don't abandon me again… Only you, my angel, only you in the world can I forgive for loving me", Juliette says to Durand, just as Lautréamont's Maldoror says of the female shark: "Now I was no longer alone in life!… she had the same ideas as me."

10. Justine, Juliette, Léonore, Eugénie

At the ages of 12 and 15, blond Justine and brunette Juliette find themselves excluded from the convent where they were educated, "condemned to isolation" and "free to become whatever they want", due to the death of their parents. But Justine is handicapped from the start: she refuses to lose her "virtue" (in every sense of the word) in order to survive, and remains deaf to the advice of her sister, who leaves her to lead a life where everything succeeds. Justine begins her career as a victim on her own. Yet Mr. Dubourg, whose name indicates his bourgeois status, warns her from the outset:

"On what grounds do you claim that rich people relieve you, if you serve them in nothing?"

In 1791, a short dialogue that disappears from *La Nouvelle Justine* in 1797 appears here again:

Oh, Sir," I replied, my heart heavy with sighs, "is there no more honesty or benevolence among men?

- Very little," replied Dubourg. "There's so much talk about it, how do you expect there to be any?"**

In 1797, to criticize revolutionaries for being, like Justine, followers of "a frivolous spirituality that nothing realizes", would be slanderous! The Terror had come and gone, and none of the surviving leaders could say, as Zamé, the philosopher-king of the Isle of Tamoe in *Aline et Valcour,* did: "the main merit of my public square is that it has never seen blood spilled." Sade rages: "*Sensible men, philosophers,* in power, turn out, in the end, to be as good executioners as their Gothic predecessors."

Juliette, "the democrat", took lessons in insensitivity in Rome, from Braschi, Pope Pius VI (in office at the time) who condemned the Declaration of the Rights of Man and the whole Revolution, but in France itself, Saint-Fond, her first friend and teacher, had already taught her **the essential: never listen to your heart.**

To advance "in the thorny career of life", you need some "putanism", which Eugénie quickly understands, escaping the vigilance of a mother ill-adapted to the new times, and asking her master Dolmancé right from the start of her apprenticeship:

"Am I enough of a whore now?"

Not very feminist Sade?

Seriously, he answers in *Isabelle of Bavaria* (The Black Queen):

"It's almost always in the ardent souls of women that the kind of courage that leads to great crimes or great virtues is ignited."

Less serious, in *La Nouvelle Justine:*

"I'd been given the bad taste of having introduced only male villains on stage. Here we are, thank heavens, safe from such distressing reproaches."

And Sade doesn't invoke heaven in vain when he writes this in year III or IV of Égalité!

LET'S NOT FORGET (AND SADE NEVER DOES) THAT THE FRENCH REPUBLIC WAS BORN ON SEPTEMBER 22, 1792, the day of the equinox, when days and nights are of equal length. **On this September 22, the celestial revolution and the French Revolution finally in tune, *the era of the French* began, *the era of Equality*. Even nature had adopted the new decimal system, obeying the agricultural calendar.** The months, all thirty days long (with the addition of five *sans-culottide* days to complete the picture), were divided into ten-day decades (evil spirits would remind us that even God had a day off on the seventh day, not the tenth), and a day now consisted of only ten hours - something every Frenchman must have found *natural*: hadn't he always counted on his ten fingers?

Juliette is revising her new calendar when, surrounded by ten vits, she asks for them "everywhere! everywhere!" and Sade saturates his text with the number ten, which the French drank until they were thirsty!

This is the context in which Dolmancé's famous pamphlet, "Français, encore un effort si vous voulez être républicains" ("Frenchmen, make another effort if you want to be republicans"), was found at the Palais-Égalité. Before having it read by her brother the Chevalier, chosen for the quality of his "organ", the Marquise sends out Augustin, her servant, because this text on equality is not for all ears!

Sade scoffs at the dreaded task the Terror had set itself: *regenerating* **an old people, uprooting** *poisonous plants*, **cutting, pruning, straightening, remaking.** He scoffs at this harassing and endless march of men borrowing their vocabulary from agriculture, ignoring everything about nature and believing they can separate, like others before them and by equally formidable means, the wheat from the chaff, the new from the old, counterfeit and useless men from healthy men, and all to establish equality... *As* for the *mother country,* to honor

Calendrier Républicain
X
Avec la participation
sans-culottide de :
Justine, Juliette,
Léonore, Eugénie...

her, let's kill the real mother or separate her from her children, because no one can have two mothers.

All the speeches of sadistic libertines are of the same flour, nightmares for philosophers whose apparently flawless arguments lead to "infamous" conclusions. How can you put up with an imitator who always turns you into a villainous philosopher?

The hatred of nature is there, in those who dream only of destroying everything in order to rebuild, remodel and see the emergence, at last, of a new humanity freed from all its original "vices". Today, others, barely elected, are taking on this onerous task and setting up vice monitoring committees comprising, of course, only the virtuous. **Vertueurs,** rather, as Laurent Dispot calls them[5].

If a "wind" blows through *La Philosophie dans le boudoir,* it's not the wind of the Terror that narrowly missed Sade's head, accused of "moderantism", it's, to paraphrase Nietzsche, a wind of thaw, madness, exuberance and gai savoir. All French people felt this springtime in 1794, when this anonymous little book was published. No more castle, no more convent, no more underground passage, just a boudoir and a day during which Sade had fun clearing up a few misunderstandings about his work.

---

5. DISPOT (Laurent), *La Machine à terreur*, Le Livre de poche, 1984.

Sodomy? Inversion? A sign of a man of power who, as the Marquise says, only takes from behind and by treachery, such is Dolmancé's inversion. "D'enculeurs l'histoire fourmille" (History is teeming with fuckers), says a burlesque line (octosyllable) in *Juliette*. Compared to this, what is the weight of the small private inversion of a man, an amphibious animal, who does no violence to anyone by flirting with the chevalier he finds to his liking in the Palais-Égalité? Doesn't the marquise define herself as an "amphibious animal"?

"I'm an amphibious animal; I like everything, I enjoy everything, I want to bring all genres together."

The joyful lie of the novelist has replaced the ferocious lie of the man in power.

Torture? Violence? Eugenie, the Chevalier and the Marquise invent very complicated and impractical ways of punishing Eugenie's mother. "I," says Dolmancé [their immoral teacher], "soften the sentence, but I carry it out, whereas your pronouncements are nothing but the effect of a biting mystification.

FOR SADE, *executing is* THE MOST BARBARIC VERB IN THE FRENCH LANGUAGE. Only states execute. When his wife wants La Coste to *execute* a small pavilion designed by him, he asks her to give up this police-exempt vocabulary and tells her that **his ideas are beyond execution.**

Nothing less realistic and less reproducible than Sadian scenes, a passage from *La Nouvelle Justine* insists on the sadness of "naturalistic" paintings:

"Ahe!... Ahe!... Ahe!..." he cries (it's his passion we're painting from life) "Ahe!... Ahe!..."

Dolmancé remains a character in a novel, and is also part of the great mystification, the great Sadian Carnival:

Mrs de Mistival, Eugénie's mother, will be stuffed and sewn up like a poularde, and, contrary to Barthes' assertion, the red waxed thread used for this purpose refers us not to sewing but to cooking, and is the detail too many that breaks the realistic and unbearable aspect of the scene.

At the end of *Juliette*, this same red thread will enable Dolmus (Dolmancé revisited by Momus, the god of satire?) to sew the "con" and "ass" of the "poularde" Justine, not to forbid access, as Lacan asserts in his afterword, but so that Saint-Florent can "larder" her after "narrowing her ways". The aim is always pleasure: the pleasure of despots who try to forbid private individuals the pleasures they reserve for themselves, the pleasure of readers who can no longer be frightened by devils with noisy saucepans attached to their tails.

Torture chambers have become butcheries and kitchens, where "meats" are palpated and prepared into "roasts", "stuffings", "boils" and various sauces according to their age and quality. Marianne, aged 7, is roasted, Justine, at the end of the course "boiled" or threatened with it, as Sade reserves supreme violence for a God or a facetious destiny. Only lightning will get the better of Justine, entering through her mouth and leaving through her vagina, and Noirceuil concludes: "We're right to praise God, see how decent he is, he respected the ass." And all this, of course, is to be taken seriously, according to Lacan, who asserts that Sade is an example of the "tragic geriatric" and lacks "absolutely [...] a sense of the comic".

Sade loved misunderstandings, and found his wife to be a "very beautiful misunderstanding"; to "get even" with Lacan, he would have painted a flamboyant portrait of him surrounded by a seraglio of houris, all with their backs to their ottomans, religiously listening to him speak to "lacan-tonnade[6]" while their forgotten bodies…

______

6. Lacan's own play on words.

Pour Monsieur Saint-Florent:
Rôti de vierge rétrécie au piment d'Espelette, Farcie au Fenouil, pommes sautées...

Sade doesn't stop short of detail that would be unbearable; on the contrary, he always adds more, and so incongruous that it's impossible to resist.

Here's an example: a hot frying pan containing a crêpe is placed on the bare loins of a woman serving at table during a banquet given by Chigi, Rome's head of internal police, to Juliet. We can almost smell burning flesh, but a little wink, a note: "Crêpe: espèce d'omelette très mince et qui se mange au sucre", breaks this effect of reality and allows us to read on. Sade always treats abuse with abuse. The lists of props and extras required to stage each orgy would ruin any producer!

A Sade so attentive to the well-being of his readers, we forgive him for often mocking us, the female readers, to whom he devotes quite a few of his notes, to assure us, for example, that he paints from life, or to count for us the (enormous) number of times Clairwil and Juliette are "screwed" during an orgy... But then, perhaps we should believe him when he asserts that our instruction, our sensations and our happiness are the sole aim of his "tiresome labors"?

How does *La Philosophie dans le boudoir* end? What does Dolmancé invite his accomplices to?

"For us my friends, let's go to the table and, from there, all four in the same bed. Here's to a good day."

The important thing is that everything is said, and said well, so that we can eat and sleep peacefully. Are we so far from Plato's *Banquet*, where the philosopher Socrates and the comedian Aristophanes sit at the same table to eat, drink and talk? All the apologies have been made, even that of salt, but no one has ever made love the subject of a table, and here we have the first challenge in the history of philosophy! Elite culture" and "low comedy" have not always been opposed, and Socrates' conception of Eros is just as "crude" as Aristophanes' beast with two backs. Before his death in prison, Socrates abandons noble philosophy for modest fable, and finally understands the "music" to which he should have devoted his life.

Is there a more innocent pleasure to be had in talking nonsense or listening to it? Okay, but why so much "foutre" and "bougre"?

11. Fuck! Bugger!

"These cruel words awakened our unfortunate lady."

Justine is at the convent of Sainte-Marie-des-Bois. She entered of her own free will, at night, on August 7, urgently seeking the help of confession. Clément refused to let her in, but she insisted, and was confessed by Severino, who passed in front of her, naked, with **"a device capable of piercing the blindfold of superstition" if it could be pierced**, but Justine, in oraison, saw nothing and heard only the speech that corresponded to her desire and belief. **Severino, with his words, "elevates" her soul and thus takes possession of her forgotten body with impunity**: always of her own free will, she follows him into the underground tunnels where the instruments of torture are hidden. Once sheltered, he finally gives up his convincing rhetoric and lets loose a "foutre" and a "bougre" that allow our unfortunate "whore by benevolence and libertine by virtue" to realize that she has once again been "a victim of her candor".

Before the Revolution, *Justine had a* single date: June 7, the eve of Saint-Médard's Day, the day on which the little rosières (the pretty Miss Vertu of the time) were elected. In 1791 and 1797, there was still only one date, but it was different: **Justine entered this hotbed of torture on August 7, the eve of Saint-Dominique, patron saint of all inquisitors and founder of the Jacobins (after the dissolution of all orders, the various clubs were named after the convent where they met during the Revolution. Jacobins, Feuillants, Corde-liers. For Sade, enclosed places steeped in such history contain a stale air that condemns their new occupants to imitation).**

WHILE THE LAST TWO JUSTINES INSIST ON THE RESPONSIBILITY OF THE EXECUTIONERS, IN THIS CASE THE JACOBINS, THEY CONTINUE TO DENOUNCE THE IMBECILITY OF THE CONVERTED, the convinced, the supporters of all the fine speeches that preach the oblivion of the lower body and concrete pleasures in favor of the higher, the distant, and make the lovers of paradise who sing the consenting victims of all barbarities and also, unfortunately, their best supporters.

At the end of his life, in Charenton, Sade had *Isabelle of Bavaria,* the abominable Queen of France, give "the" speech that, everywhere and at every time, has given the signal for battle between factions that had initially been careful to distinguish by colors or "stripes": white, red, who cares, crime always needs livery. Nudity at least has the advantage of erasing all such distinctions.

What does Isabelle of Bavaria have to say?

"Brave supporters of the good cause, could you be fooled for a moment by what is being planned today against our common interests? What would happen to us if this bloodthirsty faction took control of Paris? The squares would be covered with scaffolds, nothing sacred for such scoundrels. Believe me, the rigors we have been forced to employ up to now have only been aimed at preventing their rage by appearing as wicked as they are. If we have spilled a little blood, it is to spare the torrents they would have spilled of ours, etc., etc. Virtuous defenders of the right, etc., etc."

These are the speeches that, in all eras, electrify heads and make Armagnacs and Burgundians, aristocrats and patriots and so many other virtuous people of the same flour mingle, because **no one has ever joined the "Society of Friends of Crime", everyone has**

always fought for good causes defended by men with pleasant faces.

How does Sade respond to this kind of discourse?

In private: "Cough, blow your nose, spit, fart and sing Margot a fait Biribi" or "Va-t-en voir si j'y suis Jean… Va-t-en voir si j'y suis, Nicolas."

His burlesque "étrennes" sent from the Bastille to Jeunesse, his valet, describe him as a captain waiting to charter his ship *Le Redoutable with* forty cast-iron mullet vits "to put on the foresail, to give it a more fearsome air". Sheltered by such cannons, Sade imagines himself sailing, at last, to more clement climes: "And then I'll set sail to go cruising this spring."

To read Sade and embark safely, you need two firewalls: Spinoza and Nietzsche.

Nietzsche, who reminds us that "judgment from the point of view of tastability (it's to vomit!) is the fundamental judgment of morality" and Spinoza, that "the word dog does not bite". As for Sade, he is, above all, a novelist, and when a novelist like Sade decides to remember the anthropophagic times he lived through only to turn them into tales to frighten his nephews (this is what he writes to Gaufridy as he leaves Picpus), the nephews in

us shudder, even as we repeat to ourselves like a mantra: "The word dog doesn't bite."

If he wrote the word dog, Sade would at least manage to make it bark, so when he writes the words "vit", "con", "cul" we run away like scared little chicks and demand censors who put the sentences back in their pants!

12. Neither Left nor Right: A Novelist

IN HIS *Idée sur les romans*, SADE REJECTS THE "COMMON IDEA" THAT THE NOVEL ORIGINATED IN GREECE, the birthplace of science and philosophy, and argues that it originated in Egypt, "the certain cradle of all cults".

"No sooner did men suspect immortal beings, than they made them act and speak; from then on here are metamorphoses, fables, parables, novels; in a word, here are works of fiction, as soon as fiction takes hold of men's minds."

Gods, heroes, giants, novels, the fabulous - this is the field in which Sade excels, and his greatest pleasure is to bring back to life the giants of his childhood, the devils of the Corpus Christi processions in Aix, which shocked Casanova, who was used to the carnival in Venice - a tasteful carnival that managed to survive, unlike the giants who wore their sex on their shoulders, or the representations of all the deadly sins that anyone could mock. Casanova fled this "ferocious" Provence with all his might and, what's more, insisted that all Provençal women were nothing but shameless tribesmen.

What other origin could we give to Minski, the stentorian-voiced Muscovite, the Appenine hermit, astonished that young Juliette and Clairwil no longer know who he is or to which tradition he belongs[7]?

Minski has all the attributes of an anthropophagous giant. The purest products of traditional carnivalesque cuisine can be found in his dungeon: "blood sausages made with the blood of nannies and pate aux couilles", "quartier de garçon fort bien apprêté" and turds served for dessert in white porcelain bowls.

Minski's gigantic hypertrophy of the "lower" body: the absorption of enormous quantities of human flesh ensures a constant erection when he sleeps, walks, eats and speaks, and fifteen to twenty ejaculations in a row, so abundant and tumultuous that they drench the ceiling after killing the person undertaken by such a "tool"! Minski, the "Bande au ciel", can only open his fly to let Juliette admire the "anchovy eighteen inches long and sixteen in circumference, topped with a ruddy mushroom

---

7. SADE, *Juliette ou les prospérités du vice.*

as wide as a hat's ass" that serves as his vit. And Juliette, despite her experience, exclaims:

"- Oh, good heavens!… but my dear host, you kill as many women and boys as you see.

- Pretty much, and since I eat what I damn, it saves me the trouble of having a butcher."

Let's not forget that the guillotine had for a time been considered a highly moral spectacle, and that in the vocabulary of the time, Fouquier-Tinville was said to run "the butcher's counter" and "stock up on game" for an executioner Samson "who worked the merchandise" and was enthusiastically shouted at in the heat of the show: "Let's grind! Broyons du rouge."

Of course, he also wrote a philosophical novel under his own name, but *Aline et Valcour* is surely the only philosophical novel whose author makes it clear, right from the preface, that it also belongs to the comic genre. In this book, Sade invites us to laugh not with him, but at him, and seeks to apologize for behaving like a schoolteacher. In the preface, a quotation from Lucretius in Latin, as in the good old books that protected the untrained ear.

And what does this dangerous quote say? "When you want to make children take a bitter potion, you smear the edges of the cup with honey to deceive them and thus cure them in spite of themselves." This is a novel in which Sade treats his reader as a child to whom everything has to be explained in metaphorical language.

Leonore, the woman philosopher, follows much the same path as Justine, but when she reaches a remote Capuchin convent, she discreetly hides in a confessional for the night:

"I had no desire to go and seek asylum with these good fathers; I would have become, in their retreat, too fried a morsel for them."

Léonore knows the "absinthe" produced by the negation of the lower body, and the "honey" of fine words has no effect on her. She goes to school in the open air and on the roads, with the Brigandos and a "negro philosopher", and with the Bras de Fer gang, whose pistols, terrible voice and "cruel words[8]" have a single purpose: to remind her of her feminine duties and get her to cook. To distract

---

8. Here, no "foutre" and "bougre", "we take a fortress", "we skirmish in front of the demi-lunes", we seize "the redoubt before entering the heart of the square".

themselves during the communal meal, everyone imagines and recounts how they're going to eat this "wench", "this whore". Sade's use of the "abrégé", military or culinary metaphors, allows him to "gaslight" an account given by Léonore to Aline, his very virtuous sister, and to their mother, but he insists, in very clear language, on Bras de Fer's conclusion:

"Remember that what we've just done is just a game; I wanted to keep you merry and keep you awake."

And as if that weren't enough, Léonore also draws the "moral" of the story: "These unfortunates have just indulged in some dreadful language, no doubt, but they've done me no harm. So it will only ever be in the states proscribed by society that I will find pity and charity!"

In this book, two figures of "honorable" philosophers, "lovers" and not "executioners of nature": Rousseau, whose conversation leads Valcour to understand that a career as a novelist will enable him to "sublimate" an energy that was, until then, only a source of unhappiness for him; and Zamé, the philosopher-king of the island of Tamoé, inhabited by "the richest, freest and happiest people on earth". **The two "philosophize" in the open air, walking "under the canopy of the sky"** and exerting no constraint whatsoever on their interlocutor. Yet Sainville's presence is a worry for Zamé:

"I have but one enemy to fear," continued Zamé, "and that is the fickle, vagabond European, who renounces his own pleasures in order to disturb those of others, who assumes elsewhere that riches are more precious than his own, who constantly desires a better government, because no one knows how to make his own gentle ; turbulent, ferocious, restless, born for the misfortune of the rest of the world, catechizing the Asiatic, chaining the African, exterminating the citizen of the New World, and still seeking in the middle of the seas unhappy islands to subjugate."

There are two islands in this novel: Tamoé, the island of love, and Butua, the island of anthropophagi, the island of killing. Of the two, only Butua is "painted after nature, by an exact, educated traveler, who tells only what he has seen"; Tamoé is "only a pleasant fiction", or so Sade asserts, in 1795, after his little voyage during the Revolution, an island unknown to Cook and Bougainville.

Finally, to recover from all this seriousness, let's adopt the method used by Saint-Fond. When he's bored, he asks Juliette to serve him: **"Du cul! Du cul!"** (ass!), and to make it clear that this is a literary choice, after each lyrical outburst from Faustine, Rosine and then her lover, Juliette or Clairwil name the genre to which these words refer: "Ah! Ah! voilà du pathétique! "and when two rivulets of tears flow from Faustine's beautiful eyes, the cruel Saint-Fond, says the text, "with his vit in his hand, came to look under her nose. Oh! Foutre, he cried… Cry, mignonne, cry… here, cry on my vit!", and it's all the same tobacco, so it's easy to see why Justine, the first, the second, we don't know, was the bestseller of the day. What a rest, what a pleasure after the lyrical flights of all those virtuous tribunes, not to mention the patriotic festivities, the cult of Reason and all those highly educational and compulsory distractions.

13. The Load of Abuse has Changed Hands—Long Live Philosophy!

There is so much to say and so much to quote. **How can we end?**

Sade, in the same situation, kills his heroine to "remove the desire to continue this story", for Sade, as we've understood, writes pages and pages, and more and more pages, as his own way of fighting censorship. At the end of his life, he wrote *Les Journées de Florbelle* in his bedroom in Charenton. Every time the police searched his room, his notebooks were taken away. Ten were taken, and he rewrote thirty. The thirty were taken away, he rewrote seventy and, after his death, his virtuous youngest son had the one hundred and eight notebooks of these *Journées* burnt. They never rose from the ashes, but we still have a few pages of notes taken by an employee of the prefecture as a curiosity.

HOPITAL DE CHARENTON

AT THE AGE OF 70, SADE HAS NOT GIVEN UP ON HIS *Bastille books*. These notes specify that the work will comprise "eight dialogues, thirteen days, a treatise on morality, a treatise on religion, one on the soul, one on God, one on the art of pleasure, a project for thirty-two brothels for men and women in Paris, a treatise on antiphysics, and two novels, that of Modose and that of Amélie, which, when printed, should make at least twenty volumes".

What's new is that, at a time when the Empire has made the nobility very fashionable again, and Louis XVIII is making a comeback, Louis XV enters the Sadian "bestiary" with "a big vit and a lot of apathy".

What's new, above all, at the beginning of the 19th century, when Christianity was once again seen as "genius", is that Sade chose to depict an abbé, and an abbé whose essential characteristic is "dosing his words". Of course, Juliette the democrat, the volcano-woman, didn't mince her words.

The main title, he tells us, will be: *Les Entretiens du château de Florbelle, ouvrage moral et philosophique,* followed by *La Sainte Histoire de l'abbé de Modose* and *Mémoires pieux d'Emilie de Volnange,* adorned with edifying engravings. What's new?

The "tourbe dévotieuse" has returned to center stage, the dangerous bigots of the rights of man and equality have disappeared, philosophy has regained its lightness and is running down the road with Jacques le fataliste. In the mud, Sade can reclaim his favorite garment: his philosopher's habit. He could also refuse, with an obstinacy that astonishes some people today, to acknowledge his authorship of *Justine*. Of course, he would be imprisoned for fourteen years in Charenton, without trial, by simple decision of the Emperor's Privy Council, for having written this work, so it's understandable that he would brazenly lie in an attempt to regain free air. But one of his notes from Charenton shows him above all anxious to avoid giving arguments against philosophy "to the animals of the other world" who have returned from it, **to the "suppôts de la tonsure", to the Genlis, Chateaubriand and La Harpe who have "raged against Justine, while this book was precisely winning their case".**

Admirable is old Sade, locked up again, and who doesn't give up saying how proud he is to have written such a good book as *Justine,* during the Revolution, *at a* time when heads were being chopped off under the guise of "philosophy", nor his contempt for those who, in the

present, could, if they had the stomach to read it, take advantage of it:

"If they had paid to have a work as well done as this one to denigrate philosophy, they would not have succeeded in getting it. And I swear by all that is most sacred in the world that I would never forgive myself for having served individuals so prodigiously despised by me."

Sade is a writer who refuses to say what everyone else knows, when everyone else is saying it. He doesn't laugh with anyone about anything. Nothing could be more refreshing today.

To use the horrible monk Clément as a spokesman, to go through him to say, very simply, that the most deviant man would reform his tastes at a moment's notice if he were the master of them, and that he'd rather look like everyone else than stand out, that too is uncommonly courageous.

In the end, the only thing that depends on us and is in our power is to choose the mirror through which we look at ourselves and the people around us.

All it takes is a mirror to make a person loveable or hateful. It's all a matter of imagination.

"This brilliant part of our mind enlivens everything, and truth always below chimera,

becomes almost useless to him who knows how to create and embellish lies[9]."

"The counterfeit man also finds mirrors that make him beautiful[10]."

---

9. SADE, *Histoire de Juliette.*

10. SADE, *La Nouvelle Justine ou les malheurs de la vertu.*

Ce n'est point ma façon de penser
qui a fait mon malheur,
c'est celle des autres.

Sade

Table of contents

Best sellers Max Milo Editions

Hitler's banker, Jean-François Bouchard

Confessions of a forger, Éric Piedoie Le Tiec

The Koran and the flesh, Ludovic-Mohamed Zahed

Governing by fake news, Jacques Baud

Governing by chaos, Collectif

A political history of food, Paul Ariès

Mad in U.S.A.: The ravages of the "American model",
Michel Desmurget

Mondial soccer club geopolitics, Kévin Veyssière

Putin: Game master?, Jacques Braud

Treatise on the three impostors: Moses, Jesus, Muhammad,
The Spirit of Spinoza

TV Lobotomy, Michel Desmurget

www.ingramcontent.com/pod-product-compliance
Lightning Source LLC
LaVergne TN
LVHW051159060726
842526LV00014B/3277